Alfred's
INSTRUMENTAL
PLAY-ALONG

Classic
INSTRUMENTAL Solos

THE SPENCER DAVIS GROUP

EAGLES

FLEETWOOD MAC

the rolling stones

JOURNEY

LED ZEPPELIN

Chicago

CREAM

norman greenbaum

Wilson Pickett

YES

Arranged by Bill Galliford, Ethan Neuburg and Tod Edmondson

© 2011 Alfred Music Publishing Co., Inc.
All Rights Reserved. Printed in USA.

ISBN-10: 0-7390-7999-9
ISBN-13: 978-0-7390-7999-7

Alfred

Contents

GIMME SOME LOVIN'

Words and Music by
STEVE WINWOOD, MUFF WINWOOD
and SPENCER DAVIS

Gimme Some Lovin' - 3 - 1

4

25 OR 6 TO 4

Words and Music by
ROBERT LAMM

25 or 6 to 4 - 4 - 1

25 or 6 to 4 - 4 - 4

GO YOUR OWN WAY

Words and Music by
LINDSEY BUCKINGHAM

Go Your Own Way - 4 - 1

19 *Chorus:*

HOTEL CALIFORNIA

Words and Music by
DON HENLEY, GLENN FREY
and DON FELDER

Hotel California - 7 - 1

Hotel California - 7 - 2

ROUNDABOUT

Words and Music by
JON ANDERSON and STEVE HOWE

Roundabout - 9 - 1

Roundabout - 9 - 3

IN THE MIDNIGHT HOUR

Words by
WILSON PICKETT

Music by
STEVE CROPPER

Moderate R&B (♩ = 112)

In the Midnight Hour - 4 - 1

Alfred's INSTRUMENTAL PLAY-ALONG

Classic Rock
INSTRUMENTAL SOLOS

EAGLES

FLEETWOOD MAC

THE SPENCER DAVIS GROUP

the rolling stones

JOURNEY

LED ZEPPELIN

Chicago

Cream

norman greenbaum

Wilson Pickett

YES

Arranged by Bill Galliford, Ethan Neuburg and Tod Edmondson

ISBN-10: 0-7390-7999-9
ISBN-13: 978-0-7390-7999-7

 Alfred Cares. Contents printed on 100% recycled paper.

Contents

GIMME SOME LOVIN'

Track 2: Demo
Track 3: Play Along

Words and Music by
STEVE WINWOOD, MUFF WINWOOD
and SPENCER DAVIS

25 OR 6 TO 4

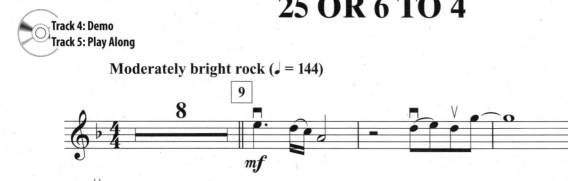

Words and Music by
ROBERT LAMM

Moderately bright rock (♩ = 144)

molto rit.

GO YOUR OWN WAY

Track 6: Demo
Track 7: Play Along

Moderately bright rock (♩ = 136)

Words and Music by
LINDSEY BUCKINGHAM

HOTEL CALIFORNIA

Track 8: Demo
Track 9: Play Along

Words and Music by
DON HENLEY, GLENN FREY
and DON FELDER

Moderate rock (♩ = 76)

(Tempo click)

Hotel California - 3 - 1

25 𝄋 *Chorus:*

f

To Coda ⊕

33 *Verse 2:*

mp

8

ROUNDABOUT

Track 10: Demo
Track 11: Play Along

Words and Music by
JON ANDERSON and STEVE HOWE

Moderate rock (♩ = 138)

Roundabout - 3 - 1

10

88 *Chorus:*

107

IN THE MIDNIGHT HOUR

Track 12: Demo
Track 13: Play Along

Words by
WILSON PICKETT

Music by
STEVE CROPPER

In the Midnight Hour - 2 - 1

OPEN ARMS

Track 14: Demo
Track 15: Play Along

Words and Music by
JONATHAN CAIN and STEVE PERRY

Slowly, expressively (♩ = 96)

(I CAN'T GET NO) SATISFACTION

Track 16: Demo
Track 17: Play Along

Words and Music by
MICK JAGGER and KEITH RICHARDS

Moderately, driving (♩ = 132)

STAIRWAY TO HEAVEN

Words and Music by
JIMMY PAGE and ROBERT PLANT

Stairway to Heaven - 2 - 1

SPIRIT IN THE SKY

Track 20: Demo
Track 21: Play Along

Words and Music by
NORMAN GREENBAUM

Spirit in the Sky - 2 - 1

DON'T STOP BELIEVIN'

Track 22: Demo
Track 23: Play Along

Words and Music by
JONATHAN CAIN, NEAL SCHON
and STEVE PERRY

Moderate rock (♩ = 120)

Don't Stop Believin' - 2 - 1

SUNSHINE OF YOUR LOVE

Track 24: Demo
Track 25: Play Along

Words and Music by
JACK BRUCE, PETE BROWN
and ERIC CLAPTON

INSTRUMENTAL SOLOS

This instrumental series contains themes from Blizzard Entertainment's popular massively multiplayer online role-playing game and includes 4 pages of art from the World of Warcraft universe. The compatible arrangements are carefully edited for the Level 2-3 player, and include an accompaniment CD which features a demo track and play-along track. Titles: Lion's Pride • The Shaping of the World • Pig and Whistle • Slaughtered Lamb • Invincible • A Call to Arms • Gates of the Black Temple • Salty Sailor • Wrath of the Lich King • Garden of Life.

(00-36626) I Flute Book & CD I $12.99

(00-36629) I Clarinet Book & CD I $12.99

(00-36632) I Alto Sax Book & CD I $12.99

(00-36635) I Tenor Sax Book & CD I $12.99

(00-36638) I Trumpet Book & CD I $12.99

(00-36641) I Horn in F Book & CD I $12.99

(00-36644) I Trombone Book & CD I $12.99

(00-36647) I Piano Acc. Book & CD I $14.99

(00-36650) I Violin Book & CD I $16.99

(00-36653) I Viola Book & CD I $16.99

(00-36656) I Cello Book & CD I $16.99

LICENSED BLIZZARD ENTERTAINMENT PRODUCT

Classic Rock
INSTRUMENTAL SOLOS

25 OR 6 TO 4

DON'T STOP BELIEVIN'

GIMME SOME LOVIN'

GO YOUR OWN WAY

HOTEL CALIFORNIA

IN THE MIDNIGHT HOUR

OPEN ARMS

ROUNDABOUT

(I CAN'T GET NO) SATISFACTION

SPIRIT IN THE SKY

STAIRWAY TO HEAVEN

SUNSHINE OF YOUR LOVE

This book is part of a string series arranged for Violin, Viola, and Cello. The arrangements are completely compatible with each other and can be played together or as solos. Each book features a specially designed piano accompaniment that can be easily played by a teacher or intermediate piano student, as well as a carefully crafted removable part, complete with bowings, articulations and keys well suited for the Level 2-3 player. A fully orchestrated accompaniment CD is also provided. The CD includes a DEMO track of each song, which features a live string performance, followed by a PLAY-ALONG track.

This book is also part of Alfred's Classic Rock INSTRUMENTAL SOLOS series written for Flute, Clarinet, Alto Sax, Tenor Sax, Trumpet, Horn in F and Trombone. An orchestrated accompaniment CD is included. A **piano accompaniment** book (optional) is also available. Due to level considerations regarding keys and instrument ranges, the arrangements in the **wind instrument** series are not compatible with those in the **string instrument** series.

In the Midnight Hour - 4 - 2

In the Midnight Hour - 4 - 4

OPEN ARMS

Words and Music by
JONATHAN CAIN and STEVE PERRY

Open Arms - 4 - 1

Open Arms - 4 - 4

(I CAN'T GET NO) SATISFACTION

Words and Music by
MICK JAGGER and KEITH RICHARDS

(I Can't Get No) Satisfaction - 4 - 1

(I Can't Get No) Satisfaction - 4 - 4

STAIRWAY TO HEAVEN

Words and Music by
JIMMY PAGE and ROBERT PLANT

Stairway to Heaven - 4 - 1

SPIRIT IN THE SKY

Words and Music by
NORMAN GREENBAUM

Moderate blues shuffle (♩ = 128) (♫ = ♪³♪)

Spirit in the Sky - 5 - 1

38 *Chorus:*

DON'T STOP BELIEVIN'

Words and Music by
JONATHAN CAIN, NEAL SCHON
and STEVE PERRY

Moderate rock (♩ = 120)

Don't Stop Believin' - 7 - 1

Don't Stop Believin' - 7 - 3

Don't Stop Believin' - 7 - 5

SUNSHINE OF YOUR LOVE

Words and Music by
JACK BRUCE, PETE BROWN
and ERIC CLAPTON

Moderate rock (♩ = 112)

Sunshine of Your Love - 3 - 1

Sunshine of Your Love - 3 - 2